Love | Flowers

& Poetry

Natalie Buschmann

BookLeaf Publishing

India | USA | UK

Made with ❤ on the BookLeaf Publishing Platform
www.bookleafpub.in
www.bookleafpub.com

Dedication

This is dedicated to whom, I am promised to. You remain my most desirable muse and you continuously inspire me to love beyond illogical capacity. Thank you for venturing through the beauty of nature, by my side and for journeying through life alongside of me. It is a blessing to toil with you and to face every single endeavor with my love, my comrade, my soulmate, and my lover. Baby, my Baby.

Preface

Altruistic love is rare. It is the epitome of unconditional love. Yet, it is integral and it is a togetherness. To be with one's muse, in love and in matrimony. To give it permanancy, to afford it a place within the fabric of everything one holds dear. It is but Poetry in motion. Love can be unrequited, elusive, daunting, waxing and wanning but it is forever fluctuating in intensity, banality, and yet... anew. It is the random weed, akin to the flower in the concret or life in seemingly dead sand and scorching heat. It thrives. Angst, softness, shelled, harsh, melodious, ugly truth, and yet... pulchritudinous. Love and Poetry are void of simplicity and you will read that here.

Acknowledgements

Jai, Ryan, and Leila... Thank you for your time and love because there is a quality there and I am ever grateful. Mom Cindy for sending me photographs of flowers to utilize and for the Buschmann clan, I love you all and feel ever welcome into the fold. Not forgetting my Dad, I love you. As always, may this find you all well.

1. Let Us Meet There

Content hearts- swell and sway
our hearts are so mute

Come hither, sit beside me
in sheer silence

Let us gander upon the flowers
amongst their swoon of sweet aroma

Can we hear them- without ear
although, their sound is near

Our minds eye- combined
so that we may enjoy their-
sweet nectar-ed wine

Come sit with me
without fear of endearment

Let us speak with the eyes

allow the melodies from our heart
strings to please-

Our souls, like the drums of time
and sand, like the drums
of lovers dance

To beats unrefined
Our love undefined- by worldly minds

Let us find, each other
in the quiet moments- of our lives

I would, give you my time
without borrow

In this, I would find not sorrow
without promise- of the undecided 'morrow.

2. Petals of The Golden Hour

Always seeking light
Forever gazing through the firmament
Poised - Tall
Determined, to lap of every ray
In their pursuit to thrive-
They embody, breath and spine
Postured to bask in the light
Giving every bit of of joy and splendor
Lighting one's path
Allotting every moment- where beauty ventures
Each sinew- each petal-
Colored, akin to the Sun
Kissed and anew to continue its glory

3. My portion | My Practice | Ye love

Permit me to provide thee, with my portion
For every bit of me, loves thee

For, Ye awakens to but discourse of thee
Thine heart and mind, speak at length

Gathering flowers-
Mustering love-
The gumption, to love thee anew

Traversing through, compartments of my desire
only to chooseth, thee

Saith, Ye
Is he naught, thy muse, thy pang
thy red blood thing, that bringeth- me still

Hither- before Lord and Lady, I bespeak of thee
For art thou, my beloved

The quill of my heart, how else would I ascribe to thee
Writing thee, before all

It is but my practice to pen of thee
O' the portion of me, 'tis full and inked in wholeness of
thee

4. Ye Bequeath Unto thee

Require four-fifths of me but beguile my heart with thy,
stillness- an unconditional bouquet
Entice me- so, where- ye cannot bespeak to the sheer
beauteous of thoust utterance
Allow it, to allure me unto silence_ thy new found noise.

5. My Dear

I am his muse, and he
my Shakespearean addiction
We celebrate one another, on the 'morrow of nights
starry succession
My dear underwrite,
why do you not bring forth the pulchritude of flowers?
How else shall I pardon you from this life of solitude?
This unbecoming life without the rouge of my gills,
my heartfelt aptitude
Serenade my heart chords
until, my fervent bestowal conjoles you
I feign ignorance for I know not of Cupid
but intimacy pierces silence
and hearts adhere
We utter matrimonios operatic hymns, captivating all
known octaves;
amidst the reverberation of howling winds.

6. Shareth, Thou Plume

We are the emphatic tide,
of loves enchantment.
Beckoning us each to each,
and we epitomize,
our heartfelt sentiment,
like Trumpeter Swans,
against the midnight light of the moon,
and the luminescent, yellowing hue of the Suns rays,
and we go about this day unto day without tedious end.
So, that we, forever sway around,
in whirls of romance,
like two caught,
in the rapture of the lovers waltz.
I utter and you utter like ripples,
that reverberate through times eloquence.
For love is upon our very breath,
and we shall forever be as this_
As those who love, undoubtedly
Because the essence of our quills,
makes for a covenant,

that is sound,
for our love,
is forever bound.

7. Fortune Cookie Poetry | Treat a friend to flowers

Every petal is unlike the other
Every leaf is not placed systematically
Anatomically from stem to bud this flower is sound
For every ray of Sun which licks its kissed surface
Vibrance can be found
Magnified particles of dew illuminate it's hue
It is a pulchritudinous thing to behold
I cannot bring you this flower but let us saunter betwixt
pathways
It requires only your sight
Yet, if you amble about slowly it will beckon you...
Ever so fragrantly
Thus, I shall treat you my dearest friend to flowers.

8. Saith The Soul

It wrenches thy soul to ponder, for thou art thy
Shakespearean Addiction

For I am some hapless fool; a Bard, fueled by the
passions of thy muse

It all but appears to be vanity and striving after unknown
illogics

But thou art thy beloved, for I petitioned before the
uncharted firmament

For we two derelicts share common plumes- mock not
the Raven which uttered nevermore

Thine heart beats some unknown sonnet breathed by
Folklore lungs through bagpipes arriving at the crux of
epic verses

For thou art thy lyrics garbed in well dressed illogics

9. Of The Heart | Asketh

This wretched thing which beats against thy ribbed
marrow_
Caged like some daunting Raven...
Rolls deep within the angst of thou moor.

Implore I, of thou, close thou ears to maidens garbed in
beauty and folklore_
For they beckon thou beneath that which is void of
mirth...
Vexatious is the nature of those who soar through the
parting of water and sky.

Hither and thither they go, enticing passion and woe_
For thou art some lone prisoner who lives no life of his
own...
Where art thou ink and verbosity boisterously ascribed.

I bespeak of thou plumes are they ready to murder and
create_
For war spare it not the wages of fugacious hearts...

For thou art no, Phoenix but a Raven shedding off the
shroud of dark.

Bring thee thou marrow so that we may partake_
Bring thee thou freedom so that we may embark...
Bring thee thou heart so that we may impart.

For thou art my beloved betwixt pain and the dark_
For thou art my beloved betwixt Sun and the Moon ...
For thou art my beloved betwixt soot and the light.

For thou art simply my beloved betwixt the embrace and
the depth of an illogical kiss.

10. Always We speak | Always We Seek

Always is a contradiction uttered from the lips of
mankind; our vitality within the confines of our faculties
are limited due to earthly death. So, do not wrench forth
like a sudden epiphany to some grand fallacy driven
loyalty as a fool would; better yet, abstain from such
mockeries made of the self and just speak within the
capacity of your humanness... because your words can be
refuted and fall short of immortality with a dying fall.

We venture more oft than we like
To and fro on the stair of Prufrock- sauntering the minds
palace
and are we like babes- bumping our capable heads
Is it not there, our forethoughts
Meandering around our thick skulls
traversing the cortex of our abysmal minds

Let us gander a bit, rolling
rolling, and what of our emotional capacity to grasp

Be it straws or grass
Are they not anatomically quasi to one another
but we gather them different

We ask much like those before us
how do we proceed, each to each
Always ascending and descending the stair
Be it heaven or hell
and to where do we arrive

Are we at the crux of the byroads, dilapidated signs
angling to and fro
I beg you courage, before every animate and inanimate
thing
Let us speakth a vow of forever, beseech I,
let us impart together, shall we be as elbows
working in unison, having tea over
decisions and revisions

Until, time ceases and whilst it permits

11. And What Are We

Whether in stillness or in motion
we cannot experience the ego, in nature
We are finite beings- on borrowed time
Witnessing infinite miracles, before the mirror of our
eyes
even in stillness, we are ever animate
We are but breath and spine

12. We Sunrise

You and I go about building and breaking down
There is a song in which, we keep

Both each to each

We disperse amongst the beauty of nature
and it sings to our hearts each to each

We gander and it provides us
splendor, our moment permeates

Ocular's, seeing each to each,
absorbing the scene, until dawns hour turns black

The night sky, bedazzles us with its starry succession
until, the new day emits first light

13. The Mechanics of The Heart

There is a mechanical hum
Ever present, but ever slight
It beseeches, in silence...

There is a mechanical tick
Ever heard, but gentle to ear
It notes, time in silence...

There is a mechanical rush
Ever riveting, but never driving
It pushes, and wanes in silence...

There is a mechanical emote
Ever felt, but appropriated
It perishes, yet thrives in silence...

There is a mechanical reach
Ever extended, but timid
It falters, yet victors in silence...

There is a mechanical heart
Ever beating, but seldom heard
It propagates, always in silence...

Perhaps, it shall go unheard
O the life of mimes
On baited, breathe
Meant only for the oculars
Delineated... In unabashed, silence_

14. Uncharted

Sometimes, you simply fall without choice, without will
because it takes but once
To gander into ocular prisms
Where inexplicable galaxies
give way to shared plumes
And much like swans waltzing against the same full
moon
A sentiment is shared within
the iridescent iris that quasi-
reverberates against the mirrored lake... Make an
implore_ I, of you and you, of I
How do we pour each to each
How far do we venture the stair
How fair we... We two who have plummeted, where the
galaxy shoots uncharted stars.

15. Chandler Pastures | Canals of

A field of wishes, just waiting to be ushered away by
hopeful breezes.
Whilst the other field, was clad with emerald clovers and
traversing
rouge colored Lady Bird's.

What a lazy day, the Sun hung low, its rays licked the
nape of our necks
kissed our movements, and hugged our presence,
if we lingered in one spot, far too long.

We meandered and frolicked on this Sun soaked evening.

We could hear the baritone of the men, bellowing out the
catch of the day.
He brags of scales and Bass, as we oooh and ahh.

As we gander at the free flowing canal, the evening
wanes and the nights breeze

effortlessly becomes bold

Ending our adventure.

16. The Heavenly Bodies

Understand, I know the sky is without limit...
But I cannot grasp the Moon

In all that I can vanquish and rewrite on canvassed trees
I cannot rid thee_

For the earthly sky would be truly bereft without Moon-
How else, can we navigate life, without thee

Be it Sailor or Hiker
Vagabond or other

Who journey's this plane of life without, Earthly
compass
Without grasping East or West

The spheres of the Heavens, shown night after night
They shoot and fall but our perception, never ceases

We are not devoid of their light

17. Ahh Poetica

Bespeak me a balladry amidst the bygones
Where Balladeer's meet under the stars
Behind the great halls of the Opera House
Where vagabonds, sing epics on the byroads of dreamt,
dreams

Bards spake into the firmament with every bit of
Shakespearean lore
Calling upon the laureates of old, for it is they, whom
we, desire to rouse
Let us wake them, for it is they, who sit with capable
Council

Whatever should we request from the chasms of their
wisdom
Surely there are great matters to which would ease are
heartfelt pangs
Why are we, so devolved, for wisdom imparts but our
humanness stumbles

We've fashioned clinquant mirrors and yet, we miss the
monstrosity standing in front of us
Mankind or mice, mankind or maggot, mankind or some
beastly thing
Paint us— dust and stars, animate us— mind and soul but
it is intellect— to which, we are undone

18. Dear | I question

Dear Penman,
hath it not been a month of Sunday's
Where art thou
Tis ye, I beckon
Let us meet at the shore
Where the sky meets the celestial bodies
Art thou still thy muse

Ye art thy, albatross
But, I wield a worthy quill
Wise ole bird, bare unto thee, thyself
For art ye, clandestine
But a shadow, a gypsy
Why dost thou remain shrouded

From whom dost thou hide
Bask in my presence

19. Muse | Genome
Creativity

The broad strokes of my quill depict you_ and you
remain my most desirable instrument.
From the oil of your natal clay, I dip fine feathers

Utilizing the ink of your crimson tide

Crafting archaic vernaculars of old, to but display you

For you are my truth untold

The marrow of my verbosity

You unfold

How else, can I sculpt every letter of your essence
The script of love, the script of life

To whom, do I look too
but the conformity of chromosomes that bind thee

Sequentially celebrating you in your entirety
Qwerty keyboards are hardly equipped

Mac lights dim and Japanese animations hush
as I articulate in kind because depth gives to image as
poetry gives to life

20. My One | Coltrane

"Every utterance leads to a silhouette of a wakeful
nightmare.., why else do we drown in whiskey and
ambient light
Whilst brass percussions propagate, proving us
melancholy n' discoursing our love, ever so vividly... Said
of Blues

Bid us a bit of blue
As Saxophones and orchestrations serenade us, operatic
hues

Blue like, Coltrane
arriving on trains of brass and arias of sound

Speak of its quickness,
for it travels solely for the heart

Propagating off the bewails of humans, fine tuned
transcending because it is the ode of the soul

Utter not words because they pale in comparison
to high hats, and harmonicas

Feline innards sprang out in unison for they, speak to the
ear
Eighty - eight keys of old, spewing love or hate amongst

The blind and the deaf and the inept
It is there for the plucking of chords and understanding

Megahertz and gut brained homo sapiens
bearing souls, be it blues or jazz

It is something that grips all

Let me dedicate a ditty to you,
My One and Only

21. Pen to Paper

Moments that passed by, only to be rewritten, revised,
and tailored because scattered etching on dead trees was
my only reprieve-

My love, may every medium be afforded to me. Be it
paint, be it ink, be it verbal captivation, or be it action in
the self same tone-

Much is derived from poetry, its ever evolving nature, its
truth splayed in motion-

A forgotten tapestry of bygone times and of Lord and
Lady, Bards and psalmists -

Of Epics and Lore
Sonnets and Prose

Idioms and quotes
Stagnant rules and Avant-garde

Whatsoever it may be-
It is the fire that extinguishes

Journals and emotive captivation
of past

22. Superstitions | Night Hike

The Constellations ever visible to eyes, amongst the dark
of the night
We sauntered amidst the the blackest of nights, for we
lacked Moon

Every sound of the Sonoran could be heard
Superstitions gaveled away

The stars alight, clinquant, yet faint
their iridescent glow, paving our way

It was then, hearts adhered, calling unto each
beseeching unto one another, imploring

Prostrated, and public
known to one another, amongst the stars

celestially bound, each to each
As banter speaks

Let us Marvel, forevermore